Everest
Ice Climbers

Written by Rob Alcraft

Contents

Collins

On top of the world

Everest is the world's highest mountain.
It's 8,848 metres tall and is located on the border
between Nepal and Tibet. It's part of a chain of
mountains called the Himalayas. Nine of the world's
ten highest mountains are in the Himalayas.

Over 470 million years ago, the mountains were
once part of the seabed. The rocks were forced
upwards, as part of the **earth's crust** was
crushed together, pushing up like
a giant rocky blanket to
create the Himalayas.

Everest is one of the most extreme and dangerous **environments** in the world. Winds are often more than 160 kilometres per hour, and the temperature can sink below –30 degrees centigrade. This hasn't stopped people wanting to climb the mountain, but climbing depends on the weather – and a weather pattern called the monsoon. Across south Asia, the monsoon brings rain and storms. But from March into June, before the monsoon begins, Everest has lighter winds and warmer weather – this is the best time to climb.

CHINA

Tibet

Himalayas

NEPAL Everest ▲

BHUTAN

INDIA

3

First climbers

The men travelling in the first **expedition** to climb
Everest in the early 20th century had no detailed maps
of the Himalayas. All that was known about the way
to Everest was from the journeys of Sarat Chandra
Das – perhaps the first ice climber. Das was an Indian
scholar who became a spy for the British government.
In 1879, he travelled thousands of miles disguised as
a **pilgrim**, making secret maps and measurements
around Everest and into Tibet.

Sarat Chandra Das in
the Himalayas in 1879

4

This first expedition was led by the British climber, George Mallory, in 1924. After climbing over 8,000 metres, he and his companion Andrew Irvine disappeared. Other members of their expedition reported a last distant sighting of the two men, high on the mountain, climbing towards the **summit**.

No one knows if they reached the top of Everest. Mallory's **mummified** and frozen body was found 65 years later, in 1999, with injuries that suggested he'd died falling. Irvine – and the camera he's thought to have been carrying, which could hold pictures from the summit – has never been found.

Mallory's equipment was found with his body.

First to the top

The first *successful* attempt to climb Everest was made by a British expedition in 1953. Past attempts had been made from the north – and failed. The group of men on this 1953 expedition used a route from the south that they'd explored two years earlier. After weeks of slow, hard progress, two climbers in the group, Edmund Hillary and Tenzing Norgay, reached the summit on the morning of 29 May.

Tenzing Norgay was a local **Sherpa** guide and the climber with the most experience of Everest.

Tenzing Norgay at the summit of Everest

He'd been with expeditions on the mountain four times before, including a group of men from Switzerland who had made two attempts on Everest in spring and autumn 1952. He'd come within 250 metres of the summit, before being forced to turn back.

Edmund Hillary was a beekeeper from New Zealand who'd fallen in love with climbing and mountains as a teenager. He was a tough and expert climber, but he almost didn't make it up Everest. At the foot of the mountain, he fell into a **crevasse** – the man holding the rope that saved him was Tenzing.

After his success climbing Everest, Hillary worked hard to help improve life for the Sherpa people who'd helped him on his climb. He raised money for schools, hospitals and even an airport.

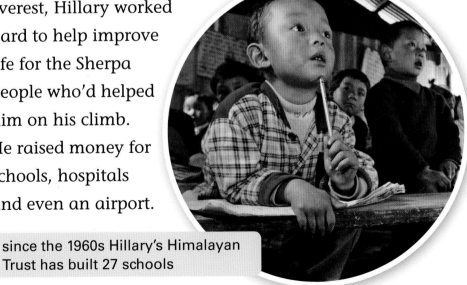

since the 1960s Hillary's Himalayan Trust has built 27 schools

Mapping the mountain

Today, climbers on Everest mainly follow routes used by the first expeditions in the 20th century. These routes are the best known and the safest ways to reach the top of the mountain.

summit – 8,848 metres

North Col

The last sighting of George Mallory and Andrew Irvine in 1924 was possibly here at the second step.

Khumbu icefall

Base Camp – 5,270 metres

Khumbu **Glacier**

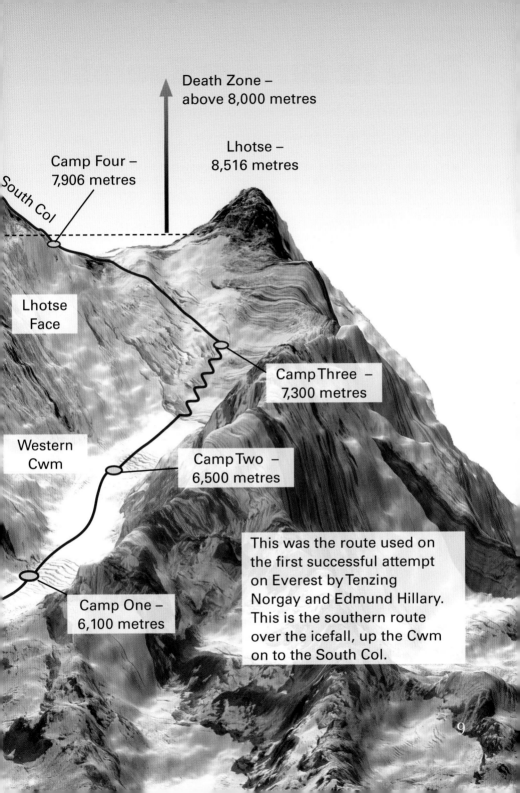

Death Zone –
above 8,000 metres

Lhotse –
8,516 metres

Camp Four –
7,906 metres

South Col

Lhotse
Face

Camp Three –
7,300 metres

Western
Cwm

Camp Two –
6,500 metres

Camp One –
6,100 metres

This was the route used on
the first successful attempt
on Everest by Tenzing
Norgay and Edmund Hillary.
This is the southern route
over the icefall, up the Cwm
on to the South Col.

9

How to survive Everest

Climbers must prepare well before they attempt to climb the mountain. The **intense** cold on Everest can kill. **Frostbite** attacks the flesh on the hands and feet. Hypothermia, where the body temperature drops, can cause confusion, unconsciousness and death. Good clothing that keeps the body warm and dry is essential – and drinking liquids that keep the body working properly.

frostbitten fingers

Each climber needs to have specialist equipment and food. On the successful 1953 expedition, the group Edmund Hillary and Tenzing Norgay climbed with took over seven tonnes of equipment, which was transported from the UK by ship in 473 separate packages. It took a team of over 400 people to carry it up to the first stopping point on the climb up Everest – Base Camp.

The constant glare from the sun and ice can cause painful snow blindness.

Today, even more equipment is needed for an expedition to climb Everest, and kit lists for each climber often recommend over 200 separate items!

Snow goggles protect climbers from snow blindness.

Warm weatherproof clothing is **vital**. Lots of layers will often include a full body suit worn over the top.

Good boots keep the feet warm and dry, and protected from frostbite.

Crampons help feet grip the ice and are essential for climbing and walking on ice.

In the high, thin air of Everest, the body and brain become starved of oxygen. There are many effects, including confusion, sleeplessness and loss of appetite. These make climbing and staying safe more difficult. Serious **altitude** sickness will kill, and most people on Everest breathe bottled oxygen to stay well.

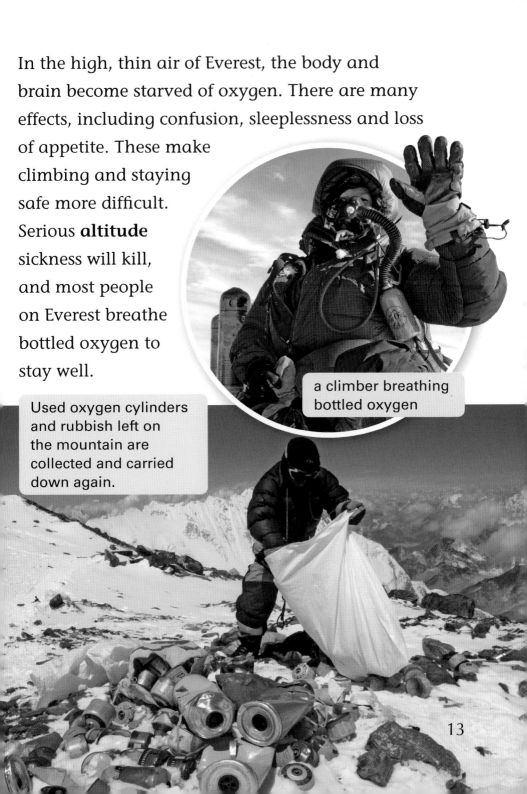

a climber breathing bottled oxygen

Used oxygen cylinders and rubbish left on the mountain are collected and carried down again.

13

Base Camp

At the foot of Everest, nearly five kilometres up in the Himalayas, is Base Camp. Since the 1950s, climbing expeditions have stopped at Base Camp, collecting and storing equipment for the climb ahead.

In the first days of Everest expeditions, Base Camp was **remote** and basic. Today, it's a bit different. Thousands of climbers and trekkers pass through, and in the climbing season it becomes a small tented town. Climbers can make a phone call or watch a film.

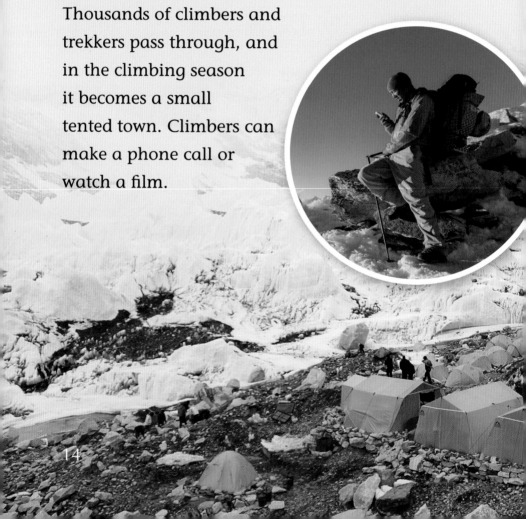

There are no roads to Base Camp. Hundreds of Sherpa climbers and **porters** are hired by groups of climbers who plan to climb Everest to carry equipment for them. Some of the heaviest gear is carried up the steep mountain paths by **yaks**.

After getting used to the thin air, the climbers who've arrived at Base Camp usually take around four days to reach the summit, stopping to rest at camps along the way.

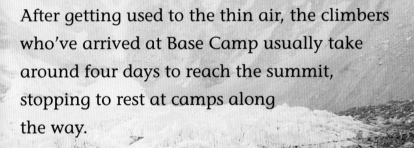

The Khumbu Glacier

Beyond Base Camp is the Khumbu Glacier – a dangerous mass of shifting broken ice, also known as the icefall. Bordered on both sides by sheer rock and hanging ice, there's no way round the icefall. The only route is through it.

At the icefall, the glacier is as deep as a 12-storey building, and it moves as much as a metre a day. Huge cracks open up in the ice, and towering blocks of ice can crash down without warning. The icefall is one of the most dangerous places on Everest.

Blocks of ice, known as séracs, litter the icefall. Some of them are the size of a house. Parts of the icefall have earned colourful and descriptive names, like the Popcorn Field, an area of jumbled icy blocks that look like giant popcorn.

Ice doctors

No expedition group would be able to cross the Khumbu Glacier without the work of an expert team of Sherpas known as "ice doctors". They're the first people to arrive on to the mountain when the season starts. Their job is to find a route through the icefall before the first expeditions arrive. They plan the route ahead from Base Camp using detailed photographs of the icefall.

The ice doctors fix metal pins and ice screws to anchor ropes on steep sections and bridge the deep crevasses and ice cliffs with ladders. Some ice doctors stay at the Khumbu glacier. They cross and recross the shifting ice every morning, keeping the route as safe as possible for the climbers and other Sherpas who use it. Other ice doctors work higher up the mountain, fixing ropes for climbers to follow.

Some of the ice doctors live at Base Camp during the climbing season.

Sherpas working as ice doctors or as guides can make more money helping with expeditions to climb Everest than they can in their villages and towns. They leave their homes and families in early March for the whole of the climbing season to work on Everest.

The Sherpa people originally come from Tibet and their name means "east people".

The Sherpa people are **Buddhist**, and the high mountain is **sacred** to them. They make prayers and offerings before setting out on to Everest, and string out prayer flags of blue, white, red, green and yellow. These *lung ta* or "wind horse flags" spread goodwill and blessings.

On the morning of a climb, the ice doctors begin their work by 6 o'clock – climbing back through the icefall to secure ropes and ladders that have shifted with the moving ice beneath. An early start is essential because as soon as the sun reaches the ice, it begins to melt and soften. Ropes can come loose from the ice, crevasses widen and the giant blocks, or séracs, can come crashing down. During the climbing season, the ice doctors may cross through the treacherous icefall 40 times or more.

The Khumbu Glacier stretches up the mountain.
The first British expeditions called this place
the Western Cwm, which is pronounced "coom" –
a Welsh word for valley. In good weather it's still
and quiet. Temperatures here can rise to a baking
35 degrees centigrade, but plunge back below freezing
at night.

Base Camp is tiny in comparison to the Khumbu Glacier. The little coloured dots are tents.

Camp One to Camp Two

Almost all the climbers use fixed ropes. These ropes are **anchored** in stages on the mountain, guiding climbers and holding them if they fall. Sherpas and porters work in teams, fixing the ropes, setting up tents at each camp, and carrying the equipment, food and extra oxygen cylinders that climbers need.

Climbers follow the ice doctors' fixed ropes and ladders on the route from the icefall all the way to Camp Two. Deep, wide crevasses – sometimes dangerously hidden by snow – cut across the route. Climbers clip on to lines that will hold them if they fall.

With the lack of oxygen at high altitude climbers struggle with relatively light packs of about ten kilograms. Sherpas may often carry two or three times this weight in supplies of food, equipment, clothing and ropes.

There are few roads in the Himalayas, and supplies have to be carried up steep mountain paths.

Camp Two to Camp Three

The climb out of the Western Cwm is up the steep wall of ice called the Lhotse Face. It's an exhausting climb of more than 1,000 metres, with a constant danger of falling. Spiked crampons must be kicked into the ice to grip at each step.

Climbers often make the journey up the Lhotse Face twice. They climb the Lhotse Face the first time to help their bodies **acclimatise** to the high altitude. The climbers then return to their camp. The second time, the climbers continue past the Lhotse Face and then climb towards the summit. The climbing is hard, and one recommended form of training for climbers before attempting Everest is to pull car tyres uphill!

An important piece of climbing equipment is called an ascender. Clipped on to a fixed rope it slides up the rope, but not down. This allows a climber to pull themselves upwards along the rope. Using ascenders on fixed ropes makes climbing much quicker and safer.

Camp Three to Camp Four

The distance from Camp Three to Camp Four is just over a kilometre – but it's not unusual for the climbers to take six hours or more to make this bit of the climb. The route is on steep slopes of ice and rock, and even with bottled oxygen, the thin air at this high altitude makes any kind of movement difficult.

This high on Everest, each breath takes in only about a third of the oxygen we're used to at sea level.

It's possible to climb Everest without bottled oxygen – but it's **risky**. Reinhold Messner and Peter Habeler were the first to reach the summit of Everest without using bottled oxygen in 1978. They spent over two months on the mountain preparing, but even so, during the final climb, they were so exhausted they were reduced to crawling.

Reinhold Messner and Peter Habeler climbing Everest

Camp Four

Climbers rest at Camp Four. If the weather is right, they set out again at midnight or earlier from Camp Four. It can take 12 hours to reach the summit, and six hours to get back down. It's safer for climbers to set off in darkness, so they can return in daylight.

By two o'clock in the afternoon, most climbers understand that even if they haven't reached the summit, they must turn back. To be caught on the mountain in darkness can be **fatal**. With exhaustion from climbing, lack of oxygen, and the cold, it's easy to fall or become lost.

Even **inexperienced** climbers can reach the top of Everest with the help of Sherpas. Sometimes Sherpas use a method called "short rope" where they lead a climber with ropes, pulling them along if they have to.

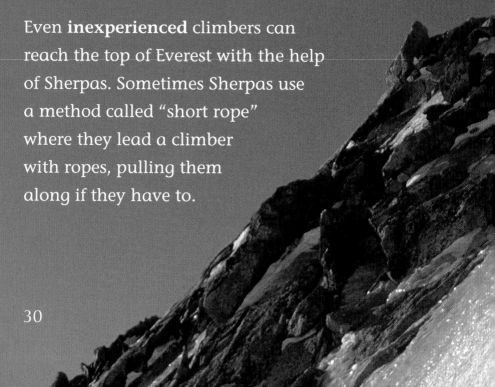

a climber using a "short rope"

The Death Zone

After Camp Four, the climbers are 8,000 metres above sea level. This is the Death Zone. Most people can only live at this altitude for a few hours without bottled oxygen. Even with bottled oxygen, many climbers – and Sherpas – experience the first signs of mountain sickness. They feel dizzy and confused, as well as severely cold and exhausted from climbing.

Sherpa people are used to living at high altitude – their bodies have adapted to the thin air that can make it hard to breathe. Sherpas can take more air into their lungs with each breath. Their blood is better able to absorb and carry the oxygen that is needed to work muscles in these conditions.

However, being tough, very fit, and used to the altitude is not enough on Everest. The work of Sherpas is one of the most dangerous jobs in the world and many Sherpas now have the chance to train in mountaineering at the Khumbu Climbing

Sherpas training

Centre in Phortse, near Everest. The training – and modern clothing and equipment – help Sherpas keep themselves, and the climbers they guide, safe on the mountain.

The summit

From Camp Four through the Death Zone, the distance to the summit is almost two kilometres. Climbers must tackle steep snow-packed ridges, and a rocky wall known as the Hillary Step.

The summit of Everest itself is about the size of a large table, and it's possible to see over 300 kilometres into Tibet, Nepal and India. Successful climbers are on top of the world, but for those who get this far they're really only halfway. A successful climb of Everest has to include getting home too.

In 2005, a helicopter made it to the top of Everest. The pilot, Didier Delsalle, used winds around the mountain to help lift him high enough to reach the summit. Normally, rescue flights only ever go as high as Camp Two.

A Sherpa called Pemba Dorje holds the record for the fastest climb of Everest from Base Camp to the summit – eight hours ten minutes!

Getting down the mountain

One of the most dangerous times on Everest is coming down from the summit – for some it's simply too far. Desperate to succeed and reach the top of Everest, some climbers keep on going when they should have turned back. With their brains muddled by lack of oxygen, tiredness and cold, some don't realise they're in serious trouble.

Having an experienced climber with you on Everest is the best way to succeed and keep safe. One climber, writing in their blog, explains: "I had a Sherpa, Chongba, with me on the 18 hours it took to reach the summit and return. Chongba, who has now climbed Everest 13 times, never left my side throughout those 18 hours."

It's good to reach the top, but it's more important that the whole team is safe, and gets home.

"Everest will always be there," says Apa Sherpa who has climbed the mountain many times, and reached the summit a record 21 times.

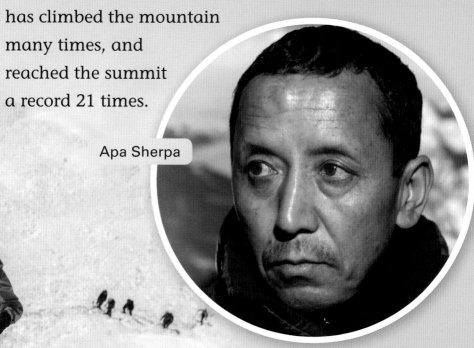

Apa Sherpa

Avalanches

All climbers have to be aware of the risks. Over 4,000 people have climbed Everest – but it's still one of the most dangerous challenges on Earth. For every ten people who reach the summit, the same number will fail – and around one more will die.

Nearly a third of those who die on Everest are killed in **avalanches**. Tonnes of sliding snow and ice released in an avalanche can crash down without warning, so where they can, Sherpas choose routes that avoid avalanche zones.

Despite all their safety procedures, in 2014 an avalanche killed 16 Sherpas. This was the worst disaster ever on Everest.

survivors dig to rescue the injured following the 2014 avalanche

Blizzards

Climbers also have to beware of extreme snowstorms, called blizzards. In a blizzard, strong, non-stop winds can reach over 56 kilometres per hour. On Everest, this can mean that fixed rope lines, which mark routes and help climbers, can become difficult to see.

On 10 May 1996, over 30 climbers attempted to reach the summit of Everest. They were delayed and, suffering from cold and altitude sickness, many were caught in a blizzard, while descending the mountain. Eight climbers and Sherpas died on the mountain before reaching Camp Four.

SCOTT FISCHER
MAY 10 1996

Earthquakes

In 2015, an earthquake **devastated** Nepal, leading to avalanches. On Everest, over 60 people were injured, and around 24 climbers and Sherpas died – three while attempting to repair the route through the icefall to allow those higher up the mountain to escape. No one reached the summit of Everest in spring 2015, the first time this has happened for 41 years.

Much of Base Camp was swept away by the avalanche that followed the 2015 earthquake.

Going home

In June each year, the monsoon begins, and wind, snow and cloud end climbing on Everest. Expeditions leave the mountain, and Sherpas carry gear down for packing and storage. Sherpas have kept the way through the icefall open for over three months, but now they head home. When they're working on Everest, most people don't see their families or children for months at a time.

Back at home, Sherpa guides get back to ordinary work with their families. Farming is important – in the Himalayas, people grow potatoes and cabbages, and tend yaks.

Sherpa children in Nepal

Climbing expeditions have made the mountain vital for work and money, but many Sherpas worry about the dangers. Sherpa expedition leader, Pem Chirri, can earn more than ten times the average yearly wage in Nepal – but he doesn't want his children to have to face the dangers of working on Everest. He pays for them to go to school in Nepal's capital, Kathmandu. "They will be able to do other kinds of jobs," he says. "They won't have to climb." For some ice climbers, times are changing.

Glossary

acclimatise	get used to
altitude	how high something is above the level of the sea
anchored	fixed securely
avalanches	sudden slips of ice and snow down a mountain
Buddhist	one of the world's major religions
crampons	metal spikes that fit on to climbing boots
crevasse	a wide crack in deep ice
devastated	completely destroyed
earth's crust	the outer layer of rock on our planet; big chunks of this crust move about slowly over time
environments	surroundings
expedition	a group of people who are going somewhere for a specific purpose
fatal	leading to death
frostbite	damage to the skin caused by extreme cold
glacier	a large mass of ice formed from snow, that moves very slowly
inexperienced	lacking skill or knowledge
intense	extreme
mummified	a body that has been protected by heat or cold
pilgrim	the name given to someone who travels to a holy place

porters	people who carry luggage or equipment
remote	not near anything else; difficult to get to
risky	dangerous
sacred	a person, place or object that is worshipped
scholar	someone who has detailed knowledge on a particular subject
Sherpa	a member of a people who live in the Himalayas and are known for their expertise in climbing
summit	the highest point
vital	very important
yaks	long-haired mountain animals related to cows and buffalo

Index

Everest blog

Getting ready to go

Remember to wear all the right gear.
It's cold on Everest!

Base Camp

This is a small tented town.

You can make a phone call home or watch a film from here.

The ice doctors

These men clear the route for the climbers.